In loving memory of Monica Lynn Petit, my oldest and dearest friend, confidant, cheerleader, and mentor. She was there for every one of my life's most important moments. It breaks my heart that she's not here for this one. I would not be a teacher today if it wasn't for her guidance. Thank you for your support through all of these years.

Rest on my friend, rest on...

It's ice cream day at Butler Elementary School. Ronald and Justin exit their classroom finishing their ice cream.

"Man, that ice cream was so good," says Ronald.

"Mmm hmmm," said Justin. "You're finished already?," he questions.

"Chocolate is my favorite," says Ronald as he throws his paper to the ground. Justin looks at him but doesn't say anything. The boys continue to walk towards the playground to play with their friends.

The next day while eating his lunch, Ronald notices that he has a pack of carrots and his favorite snack Munchos in his lunch box. "I don't know why my mom always packs these in my lunch? She knows I don't like them!" he says as he throws them to the ground.

Munchos

Carrots

LUNCH BOX

Justin looks at him, shakes his head but doesn't say anything to Ronald.

"But these are my favorite, Munchos, YUM!" continues Ronald.
The boys continue to eat their lunch until the bell rings.

Justin takes all of his trash, puts it in his lunch bag, zips it up, and begins to run to class. Ronald just closes up his lunch bag, leaves his trash on the table, and begins to run to catch up with Justin.

Seeing the mess, Cheyenne and Carla, who were at the next table, yell out to Ronald and say, "Hey! Your trash?!"

Ronald yells back to the girls, "The custodian will pick it up."

Cheyenne yells back to Ronald, "That's not OK!"

Carla adds, "If every student thought that way, our school would be a big giant trash dump!"

Ronald keeps on running.

6

7

Later that day in the classroom, the kids are making an art project. Everyone is doing a wonderful job making theirs, but Ronald is having trouble. He makes a mistake. Frustrated, he balls his paper up and starts over. He makes another mistake. He then balls up another piece of paper and tries again.

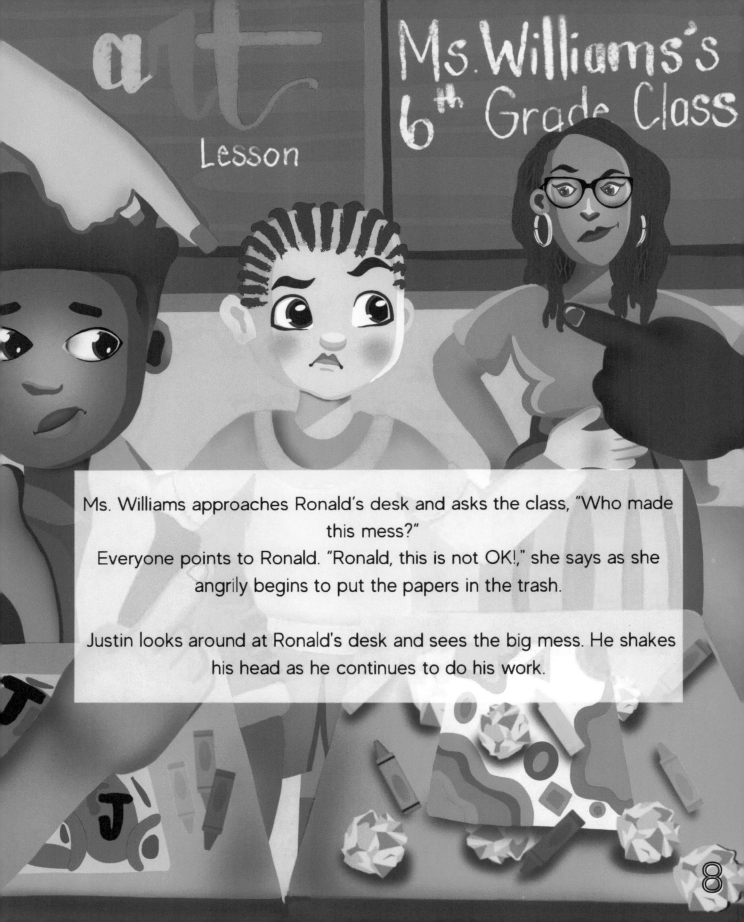

Ms. Williams approaches Ronald's desk and asks the class, "Who made this mess?"
Everyone points to Ronald. "Ronald, this is not OK!," she says as she angrily begins to put the papers in the trash.

Justin looks around at Ronald's desk and sees the big mess. He shakes his head as he continues to do his work.

8

At the end of class, Ronald asks, "Hey Justin, do you want to come over to my house to play video games after school?"
"Sure!" Justin replies.

After school, the boys walk to Ronald's house. During their journey, Ronald finishes his lunch and throws the trash on the ground like he does everyday.

Soon the boys pass by piles of litter filled with empty Munchos bags and juice boxes.

"Ewe," Justin says, "What a mess!" Ronald just looks and shrugs his shoulders as they continue to his house.

10

"Hey Mom," Ronald says as he enters, "This is my friend Justin."
"Hi Justin," she says, "Are you boys hungry?"
"I'm always hungry," chuckles Justin.
"I'll make you two a snack," Mom replies.
"Ok," Ronald says as he scurries by her with Justin in tow.

"Here you go," she announces.
The boys eat the snacks as they are playing video games.

After a few hours Justin has to go home. He begins to pick up his mess to clean up. Ronald tells him, "You don't have to do that. My mom will do it."

Confused, Justin questions, "Your mom will do it?"

"Yes," Ronald says, "She always picks up my trash, so I don't have to do it."

With a puzzled look on his face, Justin replies, "At my house, I have to clean up my own trash. Your mom doesn't say anything to you at all? My mom teaches me that if I clean up my own mess at home, I will do it out in public. That will help to keep our community clean. 'Everyone should be responsible for their own trash,' she would say."

Justin adds, "Just imagine if everyone at our school and in our community thought that someone else was going to pick up their trash for them. Trash would be everywhere. Remember the street we saw while walking to your house? The wind has pushed all the trash together. Do you like the way it looked? "

"No," says Ronald, "It looks gross!"

"Yes. Do you know how it got that way?" asks Justin.

Ronald responds, "Well I guess from people putting trash there?"

"Think about it, what type of trash did you see?" Justin questions.

14

Looking sad, Ronald realizes that he is the one who helped create the mess. He takes a big gulp of air and says, "Oops..."
"Yes, oops. You... you made that mess by dropping your trash on the ground everyday as you ate your snack on the way home from school. That's not OK."

"Do you remember what happened to the pieces of paper you left on your desk?"

"Um, no?" Ronald answers.

"Ms. Williams picked them up. I saw her face. She was not happy," implies Justin.

"Oh my, I feel so bad now," remarks Ronald embarrassedly.

"It's ok," says Justin. "Maybe tomorrow we can make it better."

"Bet, that's a plan!" Ronald eagerly agrees.

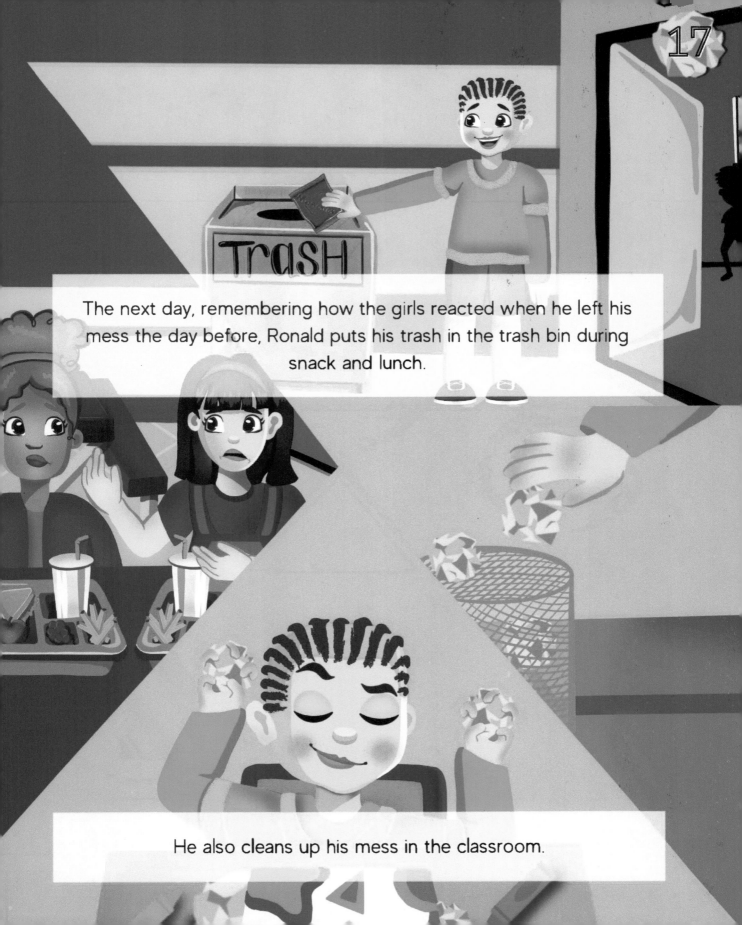

The next day, remembering how the girls reacted when he left his mess the day before, Ronald puts his trash in the trash bin during snack and lunch.

He also cleans up his mess in the classroom.

After school, the boys decide to hang out to play video games over to Ronald's house again. On the way, the two boys clean up all of the trash along the route to Ronald's house.

"Wow, I can't believe I made this mess all by myself," snivers Ronald.

"Justin, thanks for helping me clean up and helping me see how my actions affect my community. I'll try my best to never throw my trash on the ground again or expect someone else to clean up my mess." Ronald remarks.

"No worries," Justin comments.

The boys have a great time playing video games.
Once Justin leaves, Ronald begins to clean up.
He puts his dishes in the sink and throws away
any trash he and Justin had.
His mom notices.

She looks at him surprised and says, "Are you OK
dear?"
"Yes mom," he answers back proudly, "I am more
than OK! Justin helped me realize that I can clean
up my own messes"

20

Suddenly she thinks about what he said. She realizes that she has been cleaning up for Ronald all of his life because she thought that's what a good mom is supposed to do.

OH NO
that's not
OK!

"Ronald, I'm sorry I haven't taught you to be responsible for the trash you create by cleaning up after yourself. You're my baby, and I have been treating you like a baby by picking up after you all of the time. Have you ever noticed what I do with your trash?"

Recycle

Trash

Compost

"Look... I put your beverage containers in the recycle bin. I put your scraps in the compost bin. Your paper waste, which can be recycled, goes here. And, that my son leaves just this little bit that's actually trash," his mom says. Finally, I take the beverage containers to be recycled. I get money for them, that's how I'm able to buy your snacks."

Ronald questions, "Really Mom, you've been doing all of that for me e-ver-y-day?"

"Yes Son, but not any more. Today you showed me that you are capable of cleaning up after yourself and that I should let you." She pauses. "Now that I think of it, allowing you to do so teaches you to be responsible and accountable for your actions," Mom says.

"I'm proud of you Papi for cleaning up after yourself today." She then grabs him and smothers him in kisses and says, "You're right, You ARE more than OK!"

24

The next morning, Ronald wakes up thinking, "How can I help with reducing the amount of trash that is thrown away at my school?" He quickly gets dressed and runs off to school.

At lunch that day, he tells Justin about what he had been thinking. Justin says, "That's a good question. I don't know the answer, but I know who might." He looks over his shoulder to the girls at the next lunch table who scolded them about littering last time.

"Hey Girls... Justin and I have been thinking about what you told us regarding my trash," Ronald says.

Cheyenne says, "Did you know that 'eight million metric tons of plastic is dumped into the oceans each year? That's about 17.6 billion pounds — or equal to the weight of nearly 57,000 blue whales — every single year."*

"Yeah, and I also hear that in about 30 years ocean plastic will outweigh all of the ocean's fish,"* Carla adds.

*[(2021) Ocean Pollution: 11 Facts You need to Know. Retrieved from https://www.conservation.org/stories/ocean-pollu...   ...servation.org]

"We want to come up with a way to reduce trash at our school," adds Justin. "Ronald's mom has a system at their house that we think would work great at school."

Cheyenne says, "That sounds great!
"And, it's easy to start at school," says Ronald. "We can set it up during lunch time."

"Yes and the money earned from recycling can be used to buy items to help make our school look better like plants or paint to make murals," Carla says enthusiastically.

"Now you're talking," comments Ronald. "We'll call it: Mess No More!" he says as he gestures with his hands.

Mess No More

The other three kids look at him and say, "REALLY?" They start laughing. "You're a mess!"

The students work together to create a plan to start the recycling program at their school. They call it A Purpose--Giving Trash A New Purpose.

CPSIA information can be obtained
at www.ICGtesting.com
Printed in the USA
BVHW011333160323
660601BV00002B/39

9 781957 751368